DIY Survival Weapons:

Learn to Create Homemade Weapons That Will Save Your Life

Table of Contents

Introduction: Perilous Times

We hear reports in the news every single day of some catastrophe somewhere, taking someone completely off guard. There are criminals lurking in the parking garage and terrorists plotting attacks. The concept that we live in perilous times is no doubt a fact. The best way to face these challenges is to be prepared. If someone seems to be sneaking up on you out of the corner of your eyes, get ready for them to strike before hand.

Keep a DIY weapon on hand in case of just such an emergency or contingency arises. The world can be a great place, but there are a few—not so great—people and situations that can destroy your peace of mind at a moments notice, and you have to be ready for them. This book seeks to give you that sense of gravity and alertness as you learn how to create homemade weapons that may very well save your life.

Chapter 1: DIY Knife! Never Leave Home Without It!

The knife is an ancient weapon, maybe only second to blunt objects, and probably one of the first. Our ancestors were sharpening rocks and bones into stabbing implements for thousands of years before refined steel blades were even a possibility. In this chapter we will overview some of the best knife concepts, from the more primitive all the way to the complex.

Homemade Camping Knife

This knife is made to handle all weather and all situations that may come your way. And this knife will be extraordinarily useful, it's sharp enough to cut through wood, and pointed enough to tear through, and keep at bay, any potential attacker as you defend yourself.

The first step of making this knife is acquiring the steel that you will use for your blade. One of the quickest ways to get some steel for a knife is to raid your tool box.

Most classic tools such as pliers, screw drivers and wrenches are made of strong quality steel. But it is the standard, simply, file (not computer file) tool that is the most productive when it comes to creating a knife blade. To get started take out your standard filing instrument, get a black magic marker, and then use it to draw out a basic outline of where you want the edges of your blade to be.

If your hand isn't the steadiest (or most artistic) in the world, you might want to practice your knife blade outline on a piece of paper first! But however you do it, once your outline is established you can then begin whittling out your knife's dimensions from the file itself.

The best way to accomplish this is to use a tool called a belt sander (not to be confused with a Bernie Sander). Your belt sander can be used to very finely whittle your camping knife into shape. Once your predetermined outline has been fleshed out your homemade camping knife is ready to go!

Finger Clipper Pocket Knife

You may laugh at the suggestion, but you can actually turn an average every day pocket knife that we all use to trim our nails into a fairly formidable pocket knife. And no—I'm not talking about simply sharpening the nail file already inside the fingernail clippers; this is obviously to small to be of much use.

Even if you tried to sharpen the original blade it would be fairly laughable in the face of most threats. But although we are not going to use the original filing blade in the fingernail clipper, we are going to use a filing blade.

Because just like in the case o the previous DIY knife mentioned in this book, a standard sized mechanical filing tool can be used to make a decent blade. So without being too repetitive here, your first step is the same as the one that was mentioned in the first project in this book.

Simply create an outline of what you want to whittle your blade into, place it to the file, and then carve it out. After you have done this, go to your finger nail clippers and remove the original small nail file from the clippers.

In its natural state, you will find that this nail file is attached pretty tight to your clippers, and attempting to simply pull it off will most likely just cause the nail file to bend backwards without actually removing the blade.

But if you would just get out a lighter (or match) and put the nail file joint up to the open flame for a few seconds, it will loosen the grip enough that you can pull the nail file loose without any damage to the clippers or the extracted nail file.

Once removed, take this nail file and place the circular hole at the end of it (the part that was connected to the clippers) and place it right at the bottom center of your carved blade (the large mechanical file). Now take out a hand drill and drill a hole right into this hole, through your carved blade.

You can now place the hoe of your caved blade right over the hole in your clippers and screw it right in place, creating your very own homemade finger clipper pocket knife.

The Butter Knife Dagger

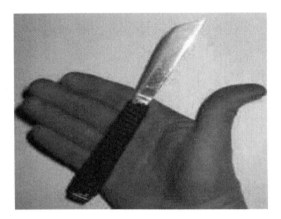

Unless you are battling a peanut butter and jelly sandwich, the butter knife does not seem like much of a formidable weapon. But if you just make a few alterations to this kitchen ware standard, you can indeed create a weapon to be reckoned with.

In order to turn that butter knife into a useable dagger, the first thing you need to do is to sketch out a basic outline of the knife you wish to carve. Now place this outline to the butter knife's surface and flesh out the dimensions of what will be your knife.

For the moment put this newly carved knife to the side, and take out a block of wood, just a plain, nondescript block of wood. Now carve this wood own to just a small little rectangle just about as big as the blade of your butter knife.

You can probably imagine where this is going, and you are right, this block of wood will constitute the handle of your butter knife. In order to complete your handle, take a sander and smooth out the corners of the rectangular block.

Now, in order to set your butter knife dagger into your handle you are going to have to get creative (of course us survivalists always do). This creativity comes into play when you hold the butter knife handle over an open flame until it is red hot. You might want to use tongs for this, but as long as you don't touch the super heated handle you should be fine.

Once the butter knife handle is heated like this, take it and drive it down into the center of your wooden handle block, the super heated metal should slide right through just like butter (well it is a butter knife isn't it).

Let this knife sit in the wood for a couple of hours until it cools off. Once cooled this DIY Butter Knife Dagger is complete. Feel free to decorate your handle as much as you want, and keep this knife in a safe place in case you might need it!

Chapter 2: How to Make Your Own Bow and Arrows

The Bow and Arrow is an ancient yet supremely effective and efficient weapon. With a good bow and arrow you can make sure that enemies never get the jump on you, in fact if your aim is good enough, they will never even get anywhere near you! In this chapter learn how you can make your own frighteningly effective bow and arrows from scratch!

Standard Wooden Bow and Arrows

The bow depicted here can be quickly assembled just from natural material gathered from the environment. To start out, grab up a piece of sapling, about 2 inches in diameter and strip off the bark until the wood is bare.

Now get out a good knife (like the ones mentioned in the previous chapter!) and use it to trim and carve down the wood until you have a thick and sturdy mid section that narrows down to two skinny termination points a the ends of the bow.

This is the basic frame up of your bow, the thicker mid section is your handle that you will use to hold the weapon, and the narrow termination points are where you will place your bow string.

And speaking of which, you are going to want to take out your knife and cut out two notches, one at each end of your bow, cut them about half of an inch deep and about one inch away from each end point of the bow. You will thread your bow string around these notches.

If you have nothing else, fishing line actually works as a wonderful form of bow string, just go ahead and tie one end of it to the top end of the bow. One this is securely tied to the top end of the bow, hold the bow steady with one hand while you use your other hand to guide the string and bend the bow back, while you tie the other end of the string to the bottom of the bow frame.

You should bend it back enough to make just a slight curve in the bow, don't over do it, and just let the bow naturally bend slightly as it the wood adjusts to the pressure of the tied string.

With your bow in place you can then move on to make your arrows. For your arrows collect a bunch of thin wooden tree limbs and cut off all of their bark. Next, carve the ends of these thin sticks to nice and sharp points. You might want to also put the tip over a good strong campfire just to harden its point.

After you have done this put a hairline split at the opposite end of the stick, this will comprise the arrow shaft that will rest on the bowstring when you are getting ready to fire off the arrow. It's as easy as that my friends, you now have yourself a reliable bow and arrows ready for anything that may come your way.

The DIY Improvised Crossbow

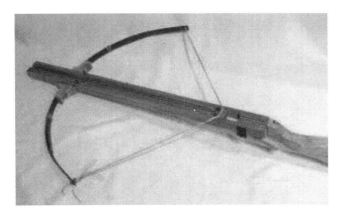

Crossbows are powerful, and before the invention of modern firearms, these weapons held the record for fastest projectile capability. Their simple design doubles the speed of arrows hurled from them, and can prove to be your best friend in a dangerous situation.

To begin the creation of your DIY Improvised Crossbow you need to start off with a design similar to the standard bow in the above mentioned project.

This means getting a tree branch, scraping off all the bark and whittling it down to where the mid section is thicker, while the wood narrows down toward each end point.

After this cut your notches into the end points of the brow frame just like you did in the previous project, an string your bow. Next pick up a large, flat piece of would, for the sake of this project lets use thick, flat tree branch. It should be about 3 inches wide, at least 2 inches thick, and about 2 and a half feet long.

This piece of wood will be the platform for your crossbow, put this piece of wood down on a flat surface and then put your standard bow on top of it. Now just take out a couple of nails and nail through the thick mid section of your bow, on into the wooden platform of your crossbow, connecting these two pieces together.

You can now pick up this entire assembly, and aim with ease, firing arrows in rapid succession from the platform of this completed DIY improvised Crossbow.

The Bicycle Rim Bow

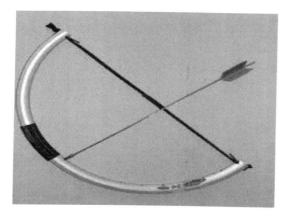

If you are biking it down the road during the zombie apocalypse and your bike gets a flat tire, before you completely ditch your ride you should consider turning your bike's wheel into a bow!

Because it just so happens that the metal rims of bicycle wheels makes for the perfect bow frame! To get started remove your bikes rim from the bicycle, once removed, take out a saw and use it to cut your rim completely in half, leaving behind a perfect half circle of the rim.

Next, take a piece of fishing line or nylon cord and run it through the rim holes conveniently located on the top and bottom ends of your bow rim. Tie your bow string material off at the ends. You can then craft some wooden arrows in a manner similar to what was mentioned earlier in this book or you could get even more creative, constructing plastic and metal projectiles.

The beauty of the bicycle bow is that it is super strong without losing any of its flexibility. This means you can use much heavier arrows without losing any aerodynamic ability of the bow. Now all you have to do is imagine yourself in some dystopian mad max landscape wielding this true survival weapon! This thing is the real deal!

Coat Hanger Bow and Arrow

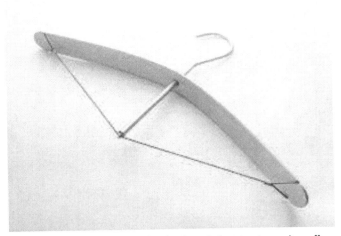

I know this one seems absolutely absurd, but trust me, it really works! And all you will need in order to do this survival weapon DIY is a plastic coat hanger, a kitchen knife (or perhaps your own DIY one), masking tape, scissors, an empty toilet paper roll, and an old shoestring (talk about shoestring budget).

First lay your coat hanger down on a flat surface (such as your kitchen table, workbench, floor, and etcetera).

Next, you are going to want to take out your scissors and snip through the coat hanger in three strategic places; the left corner, the right corner, and right at the top of the triangle tip of the frame just below the hook, severing the hook of the hanger from the bow frame completely. After you have done this grab up that empty piece of toilet paper roll (clean toilet paper roll please!) and cut it right down the middle long ways.

Attach this sliced toilet paper roll around the top corner of the bow frame where the hanger's hook used to be, this will constitute the hand grip of your bow. Roll the toilet paper roll up tightly over the bow frame and tape it in place with your masking tape.

Now take out your piece of shoestring (yes, simple, common, everyday shoestring) and cut out a section approximately the same width as the space between the hangers severed end points.

Now attach the ends of this length of string to the endpoints with your masking tape. Your Coat Hanger Bow is now complete! For arrows you can fashion simple wooden arrows as described previously in this book or even thin metal projectiles from additional wire coat hangers.

Chapter 3: From Ordinary Stick to Extraordinary Weapon

It takes some real DIY spirit and ingenuity to take a bland, ordinary stick and turn it into an extraordinary weapon. But rest assured; it can be done! And this chapter has the projects to prove it!

The Caveman Club

As the name of this survival weapon DIY just might imply, this one harkens back to the days of our ancient ancestors. Because by all accounts one of the first weapons to ever by conceived was probably a big thick club that the ancients used to hit each other over the head with! But a good club is still something that can be refined, and this DIY shows you how!

To get started take a thick tree branch—were talking about 4 inches in diameter—and with your knife whittle the stick down from the bottom to the top, with the wood being narrower at the base.

Soon your stick should have a nice thick tip (good for clubbing heads) and a narrow handle at the bottom (good for holding). It's as simple as that folks! It really doesn't take a caveman to build a great caveman club!

The Weaponized Walking Staff

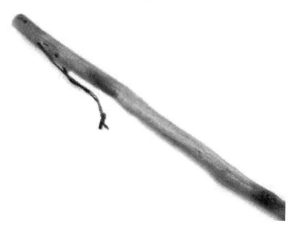

A former U.S. President once said, "Talk softly, but carry a big stick", well with this little DIY you can do just that! You need to use a tree branch that can reach up to your waist when stood up on the ground. Begin whittling this tree branch down, until all the bark is off and the wood is streamlined and perfectly smooth, just like a basic walking stick.

Now here is where you can get a bit creative. Take your knife and carve some jagged edges on the top face of the walking staff. These edges will be an effective weapon if you ever have to take your staff and strike it against the side of an attackers head! This staff can be very dangerous, so of course, only use it if you or your loved ones lives are being threatened.

The Homemade Throwing Spear

Spears have been with us for a long time and they have proven their worth over the millennia. And when you can throw them with precision at moving targets they are worth their weight in gold. You never know if you might be in a dangerous situation in which a deadly animal or person is in pursuit and you need to launch a projectile to stop your aggressor in its path.

It may sound like a joke to some, but spears have been used in some parts of the world to stop attacking lions and charging elephants in their tracks, so no matter what you might think, the capacity of these weapons are still very great, and could save your life if you ever find yourself faced with a dangerous aggressor.

To get started on your own homemade throwing spear all you will need to do is to gather up a fairly green piece of sapling off of a tree, make sure that it is about as thick as a broom handle, and strip all of the bark from the wood. Now trim the stick until it is about 5 feet in length.

Take your knife and use it to carve one of the ends into a sharp point, you can then put an open flame (either a lighter or campfire does the trick just fine) letting al moisture leave the tip of your spear, so that the sharp end becomes hardened and solid. And simple as that, your throwing spear is now ready for action.

Chapter 4: Everyday items as Emergency Weapons

In reality; just about anything can be turned into a weapon, you just have to know how to use it. If you are standing in line at the gas station for example—holding onto your can of coca-cola when a masked gunman charges in and orders everyone to the get on the ground—if you launch that can of pop as hard as you can, striking the assailant right in the face with it, you could easily neutralize the attack.

Launched hard enough the innocuous, everyday item of a coke can could smash the gunman's nose into several pieces instantly incapacitating him with pain, if not knocking him completely unconscious upon impact. The gun would most likely fall from the attacker's limp hand and his robbery attempt would be over, without you or anyone else having to "get on the ground" or listen to any other life threatening commands from the attacker.

It may not be readily apparent to the untrained observer, but there are potential sources of weaponry all around us if you know where to look for them. In this chapter we are going to explain how everyday items just like this can be turned into emergency weapons if it were ever to become necessary. So keep reading, and keep your eyes peeled, because we're pulling our DIY weapons right out of the thin air with this one!

Pen or Pencil

We often have them right there in our pockets, but when push comes to shove, not very many even consider the possibility of turning them into emergency weapons of survival. But they should, because these simple utensils if used right can easily inflict serious, if not lethal damage to an attacker, thereby saving your own life in the process.

If a mugger pulls a gun on you and demands that you hand over your wallet "right now" as you reach in your pocket and feel a pen brush against your fingertips grab hold of it. While still pretending to comply to the mugger's demands, pull that ink pen out with lightning speed and without holding back, drive it deep into your attacker's eye.

He will be in so much pain (and shock) that he will probably forego the attack completely and double over on the ground like a frightened roly-poly bug attempting to pathetically defend himself against the person whom he was attempting to rob just moments before! As mentioned earlier however, this everyday item used in such a manner could be quite lethal, so only use it if you truly feel that your own life is in danger!

Nine Volt Battery

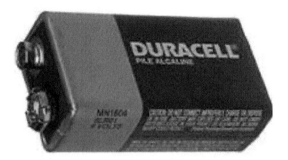

This one might have surprised you, and perhaps you think I'm suggesting you throw a battery at someone? No of course not. Why throw it when you can shove it down there throat? Does it sound crazy? Yep, crazy enough to work! Using this everyday item in such a manner works well if you are in close quarters with an attacker. If someone is manhandling you and attempting to over power you, give them the surprise of their life!

Instead of trying to grapple with them, while their hands are busy trying to put you in a headlock, or whatever they are trying to do to you, reach up, find the assailants mouth and force that rectangular little nine volt battery down their throat! No one in their right mind (unless maybe they read this book) would ever imagine that you would do something like that!

As the battery gets lodged deep in their windpipe their immediate reaction will be to let you go and wildly run away from you as they horribly choke on the obstructive, 9 volt piece of horrible pain, jammed in their throat.

Along with choking on the battery stuck in their windpipe, as fluid builds around the object, they will probably start getting shocked by the battery as well! If the attacker lives through this experience, no matter how much of a bully he was before, this run-in will scare the crap out of him so much, he will never think of bullying someone like that ever again!

Hot Coffee

This everyday item turned weapon has actually seen quite a bit of use by gas station clerks against would-be armed robbers. Boiling hot coffee does tend to diffuse the situation. It distracts, inflicts pain, and takes away the confidence of the assailant. This one really is rather self explanatory, and it is more of a weapon of convenience more than anything else.

Since none of us go around carrying our double espresso with the idea that we might have to use it for self defense (nope, I drink that stuff), this emergency survival weapon is only a go-to form of self defense if it happens to already be on hand.

If you just walked out of star bucks with a cup of Joe in your hand and someone shoves you from behind and starts talking smack, feel free to greet their belligerence with a splash of boiling hot coffee to the face.

Plastic Bag

If you are walking to your care after a grocery run and someone attacks you in the parking lot, take one of your plastic grocery bags and jam it over the assailants head. Pull tightly on the handles making the bag nice and tight. The attacker will quickly begin to suffocate with his air supply cut off, and his vision will be compromised, unable to see through the thick plastic.

This is just a temporary diversionary tactic however, since any assailant, after he gets over his shock and mutters, "what the f * * *?" will be able to easily take the plastic bag off.

But the five seconds that he struggle to do this, has bought enough time to run away from your would-be attacker and the commotion that the brief struggle garnered no doubt has generated enough public interest that the assailant will probably abort his plan and make a run for it himself to avoid all the sudden publicity!

Belt

Yep, the everyday item of the belt is not just for old-school disciplinarian parents, it can also be weapon of self defense against a random aggressor. This one obviously would not work too well against a sudden attack, since you can hardly take the precious time needed to undo your belt while your enemy is viciously pummeling you in the head with his fists.

But if you are in a threatening situation with just a little bit of time on your side, such as during a robbery situation in which you are a bystander, you can quickly take the belt off and potentially use it against the robber as a survival weapon. And a belt buckle across the face is no doubt a very painful and frightening prospect for anyone.

In using a weapon like this, the best strategy is to start striking the gunman as hard and as aggressively as you can without backing down, they will be so overwhelmed in attempting to ward off your blows they won't even be able to use their weapon. So yes, in a situation like this, if your life is in danger, you just might want to reach for your belt.

Screwdriver

This one is similar to the pen or pencil everyday item turned weapon, and it is pretty self explanatory. Just imagine you are out there trying to tighten up your side mirror on your car with a screwdriver when some drunken bozo comes up out of nowhere and pulls a knife on you demanding your car keys, well guess what?

You may not be bringing a knife to a sword fight, but *you can* bring a good Philips screwdriver to a knife fight.

And even while your back is turned and the clown is menacingly breathing down your throat telling you, "give me your keys" clutch the screw driver hard in your hand, spin around, and without warning, lunge that screwdriver with all your might, deep into their chest. The attacker will no doubt drop to the ground in horrible pain, and you will live to tell the tale.

Conclusion: Stay on Guard

There can be no doubt that we live in a dangerous world, and you just might win the unlucky lottery someday and find yourself in a life threatening situation. The key to surviving such potentially traumatic experiences is to not think of them as such.

Don't get caught up in the emotion of the moment, instead clear your mind, grab your chosen weapon of survival and bash your attacker senseless with it so you can live to see another day! Thank you for reading this book, I truly hope it can help you protect yourself and your family! Helping you to stay safe, and stay on guard!

Made in the USA
Las Vegas, NV
15 September 2021

30382103R00017